stairs

architectural details

Imprint
The Deutsche Bibliothek is registering
this publication in the Deutsche National-
bibliographie; detailed bibliographical
information can be found on the internet
at http://dnb.ddb.de

ISBN 978-3-938780-46-6 (Hardcover)
ISBN 978-3-938780-65-7 (Softcover)

© 2008 by Verlagshaus Braun
www.verlagshaus-braun.de

1st edition 2008

Editor:
Markus Sebastian Braun
Editorial staff:
Julia Goltz, Annika Schulz
Translation:
Alice Bayandin
Graphic concept and layout:
Michaela Prinz

stairs

architectural details

BRAUN

contents

6 stairs - step by step

10 amsterdam
16 athens
24 barcelona
32 berlin
44 brussels
50 budapest
54 copenhagen
64 cracow
70 istanbul
76 lisbon
84 ljubljana
92 london
102 paris
110 prague
118 riga
124 rome
130 stockholm
136 st. petersburg
140 vienna
146 vilnius
152 zurich

158 photographers index

berlin, schiffbauerdamm 25

stairs – step by step

In architecture stairs are a connecting space consisting of steps which joins the various levels of a building, mostly on its interior. Stairs have a minimum of three steps, and are bordered on one or both sides by a secured banister or a handrail. In classic wood or stone stairs treads, or steps, are horizontal surfaces whose front tread edge rests at a vertical distance above the tread end of the step below. The inclined structural element carrying the step sequence, and into which the steps are cut on their right and left is called a stringer beam, or just stringer. The casing at the point at which the wall running along the stair meets the tread is called the trim.

The earliest stair, in use already in the early Stone Age, was the so-called climbing trunk which consisted of a tree trunk placed into a diagonal position with branch stumps serving as steps. This structure evolved into a single-trunk ladder with notches to serve as steps; this form of stairs is still in use on the islands of Oceania. Wood was used as the primary stair-building material for a long time, and was fashioned into the first wooden stair with secured steps, resulting from treads being housed into ladder stringers. Stone steps, originally made of hewn stone slabs and with variable step rise, proved to be more secure and resilient to external elements, and established themselves quickly. Use of additional construction materials like brick, reinforced concrete, wrought iron, stainless steel, glass or grating has given stair design complete freedom.

A look in any architectural guide reveals an endless row of terms denoting different stair types and their structures. An extremely practical solution from the point of view of space economy is the spiral staircase. It primarily enables going up and down in towers, but finds elegant use today in galleries and topmost stories within closed spaces. Because their treads narrow toward the center of their rotation, special care is urged while going up and down the spiral. The double-winding or double helix stair was discovered by the genius Leonardo da Vinci. These stairs have two "arms", and their entrances and exits begin and end at a 180-degree orientation to each other, making this staircase a textbook example of "discreet architecture". The persons walking along different arms can avoid meeting or all visual contact to each other. The most famous example of this type of stair is found in the Château de Chambord in the Loire Valley in France.

Countless historical and cultural curiosities can be found examining the stairs' construction. To ensure that you can start your climb up the stairs with the right foot and leave the last step with the same sole, all stairs in ancient Rome were built with an odd number of steps. It is indeed important to start a good day "on the right foot". Winding stairs in castles always turn to the right. When it was necessary to protect the upper chambers during an attack, the shaft's orientation prevented it from getting in the way of the protector's sword, drawn usually from the right, and had the opposite effect on the person attacking from below.

There are some record breakers to be found in the world of stairs. The tallest stairs in the world rise to 1,540 meters and count 6,000 steps. They are found on the holy Tai Shan Mountain in China. The world's longest stairs have 11,674 steps and lead along the Swiss Niesenbahn, the longest funicular in Europe. The widest stairs lead from the fair grounds to the new exposition area in Hanover. The longest indoor stairs in the world reach the viewing platform in the CN Tower in Toronto and have 2,570 steps.

The stairs' central role in connecting different levels of a building (in early architectural dictionaries the stairs are counted as "main parts of a house") raised questions about their safety. A handrail is often not enough to prevent slips on wet wood or stone stairs or falls down stairs that are too steep. The Economical Encyclopedia from 1773 published by Johann Georg Krünitz already demanded that a "comfortable stair", especially in consideration for "old and heavily built" persons, have a platform or landing for rest following every 10 or 12 steps, because a lack of such would overly strain bones and musculature. A landing is also necessary "in case a person slips or makes a false step that he does not fall the entire length of the stair, for such a fall on a steep stair often has dangerous consequences". This foreseen danger to this day cannot be avoided completely. Falls from stairs and ladders are listed as by far the most common cause of deadly household accidents that claim several thousand lives a year in Germany alone. Spectacular falls down stairs can be found throughout the annals of history. In 1556, exactly one year after taking the throne after an exile lasting several decades, India's great Mogul Humayan fell to his death down a set of stairs. Supposedly, in his rush to be in time for prayer, he got entangled in the hem of his dress. The misfortune-plagued subjects of the margrave Eduard Fortuna of Baden-Baden, famed for his counterfeiting and robbery, saw his drunken fall down the stairs in his Kastellaun castle in 1600, which resulted in a broken neck, as a just punishment from God. On the other hand, the 1966 deadly fall of the opera star tenor Fritz Wunderlich was deeply bemoaned. The alarming psychological state of the famous heir to the Spanish throne Don Carlos was attributed to his fall down stairs, which occurred in the course of an unsuccessful romantic adventure, and put him in a comatose state for quite some time.

With their draft channels and burning steps, fires in stairwells cut off vital escape routes for occupants of upper floors. For this reason, infernos in hotels and high-rises lead to catastrophes with countless victims in spite of modern safety precautions taken in stair construction of public buildings. Catastrophe films have also borrowed from the subject of burning stairs, and not only following the September 11th terrorist attack on the Twin Towers. In the film version of Umberto Eco's In the Name of the Rose, the fire of the labyrinthine wooden steps in the mysterious monastic library reaches nearly apocalyptic proportions.

Joining and crossing of levels as well as rising to a higher plane characterize the cultural and historical meaning of stairs. If the column represents the Earth's reaching out to the heavens, steps symbolize the ascent that man accomplishes himself by reaching for a higher level. The step pyramids built by the third dynasty of Egyptian pharaohs, which included pharaoh Djoser, were constructed to symbolize the world mountain which, like the sacred mountain Meru in Indian mythology, marked the center of the universe and was closely connected with higher powers. The dangers and miscalculations of the attempt to rise to the sacred heights are known to us from the story of the Tower of Babel told in the Old Testament. The subject of the Tower of Babel legend are Mesopotamian step pyramids, or ziggurats, found in the earliest urban centers Ur and Uruk. Ziggurats comprise of stacked platforms, the highest of which forms the temple for the respective main god. The step pyramid of the construction-obsessed Babylonian king Nebukadnezar II was over 90 meters high, and it indeed is the "Tower of Babel". Unlike its portrayal on the famous Pieter Brueghel canvas, the stair did not wind around the tower, but surrounded by side stairs, one main stair on the pyramid's front led to the top levels, producing an overall effect of eminence. However such a high, winding exterior stair characterizes the spiral minaret Malwiya in Samara, located in present Iraq, whose design was based on that of the ziggurat.

The ancient civilizations of Mesoamerica also built immense central stairs on the front of their temples. These led to high platforms, where bloody human sacrifices were made. The number of steps often followed extremely precise calendar calculations for determining the cycles of the year and harvest seasons. The Chichen Itza Maya pyramid in Mexico had four stairs with 91 steps each, all ending with a common step at the top and adding to a total of 365 steps, one for each day of the year.

Since steps hewn out of stone were featured in Antiquity's amphitheaters, stairs have been used not just for ascending, but also as places of cultural events and leisurely relaxation. In many cities, especially in southern countries, stairs in front of churches are the favorite meeting places for both young and old. The best example of stairs taking on this function are Rome's Spanish Steps, or Scalinata di Trinità dei Monti, which also serve as the stage for one of Italy's most prestigious fashion shows, Alta Roma, and as the backdrop of countless films.

In this sense, stairs have always had and have until today preserved an artistic and symbolic significance which far exceeds their practical usefulness as a level-joining architectural element.

Markus Hattstein

amsterdam, stationsplein

above left, above right, below left, below right: amsterdam, prinsengracht 340, 342 | herengracht 460 | oudezijds achterburgwal 237 | nieuwe westerdokstraat 156-194

amsterdam, nassaukade 380, 381

athens, agios nikolaou

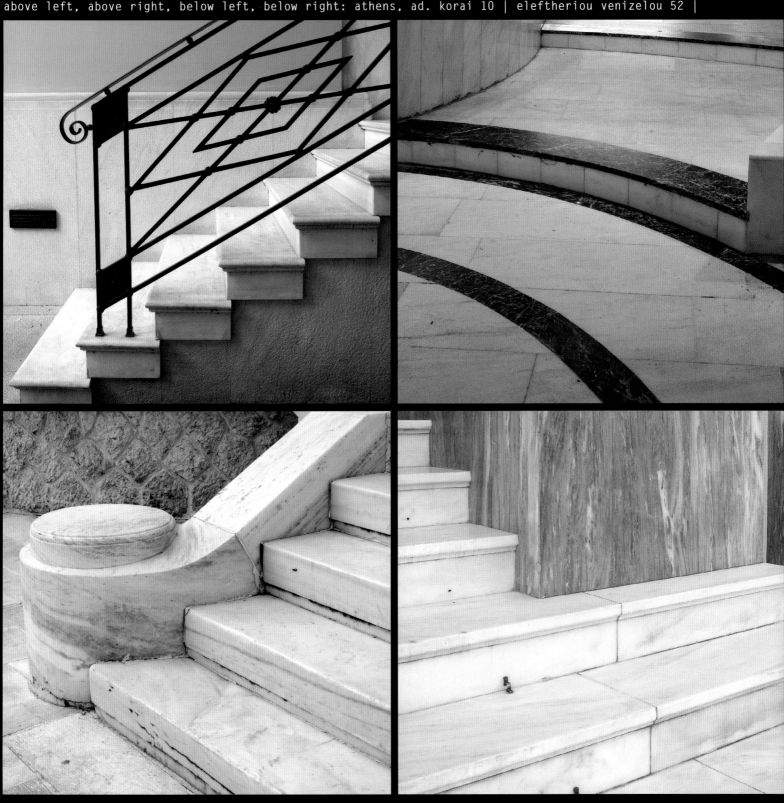

above left, above right, below left, below right: athens, akropolis | anafiotika 3 | akropolis | akropolis

athens, akropolis

athens, filellinon 12

above left, above right, below left, below right, right: athens. 28 oktovriou 55 | peiraios 100 | epicharmou 23 |
stadio irinis kai filias | national library

barcelona

barcelona, passeig marítim de la barceloneta

avenida marques de comillas 6-8 (caixa forum) | plaza del tibidabo 1 (temple del sagrat cor) | plaza del rei 2 (palau reial)

above left, below left, right: barcelona, baixada de la gloria 4 | passeig de gracia 43 (casa batlló) | calle mallorca 401 (sagrada família)

barcelona, avenida marquès de comillas 13 (poble español de montjuïc)

barcelona, paseo de gracia 92 (casa milá)

carrer d'olot 7 (parc güell)

berlin, hinter dem gießhaus / unter den linden 2 (deutsches historisches museum)

left, above right, below right: berlin, am friedrichshain 34 | linkstraße 10 | linkstraße 10 | linkstraße 10

berlin, stralauer platz 34 (energieforum)

berlin, schiffbauerdamm 25

marlene-dietrich-platz | paul-löbe-allee

above left, above right, below left, below right: berlin, zimmerstraße 100 | sony center | zimmerstraße 19/19a | köthener straße 30

berlin, cora-berliner-straße

berlin, behrenstraße 74

above left, below left, right: berlin, linkstraße 10 | potsdamer straße 47 | zimmerstraße 19/19a

berlin, zimmerstraße 19/19a

brussels, rue du taciturne 1

above left, above right, below left, below right: brussels, parlement européen | rue de la revolution iv | boulevard de l'europe | rue d'ardenne 21

brussels, bruxelles-midi

brussels, conseil européen

budapest

budapest, gellért bath

above left, above right, below: budapest, deák ferenc utca 11 | nemzeti színház | mücsarnok

budapest, műcsarnok

copenhagen

49 M

2,9 M

copenhagen, havneparken

copenhagen, kalvebod brygge 51-53

copenhagen, kalvebod brygge 51-53

above left, above right, below left, below right: copenhagen, artillerivej | kalvebod brygge 43 | teglholmsgade |
islands brygge 52

copenhagen, kalvebod brygge 35

copenhagen, kalvebod brygge 13

RESIDENTS ONLY
VIDEO SURVEILLANCE | VIDEO-OVERVÅGNING

cracow, ulica ogrodowa 4

above left, above right, below left, below right: cracow, kraków główny | plac kolejowy 1 | wawel | ulica mei-
selsa 22

cracow, ulica lubicz 1

cracow, ulica golebia 15

ulica szewska 22

istanbul

istanbul, h'davendigar caddesi

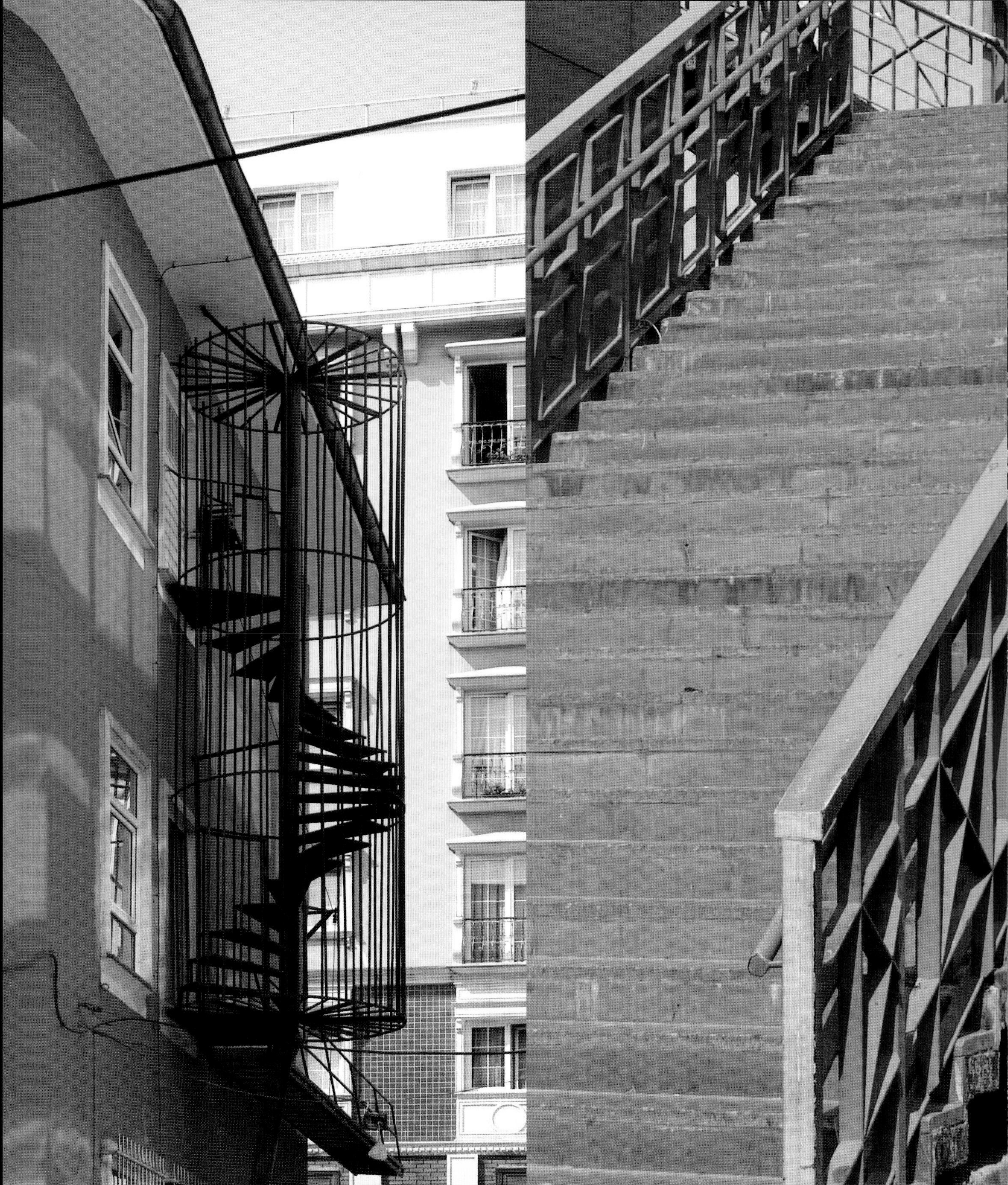

left, right: istanbul, h'davendigar caddesi | kennedy caddesi

istanbul, ayşe kadın hamamı sokak

73

istanbul, ciragan caddesi / ciragan sarayi (kempinski hotel)

above left, below left, right: istanbul, soğuk çeşme sokak | ayşe kadın hamamı sokak | tavukhane sokak

lisbon

lisbon, parque das nações (parque expo 98)

lisbon, avenida sidónio pais

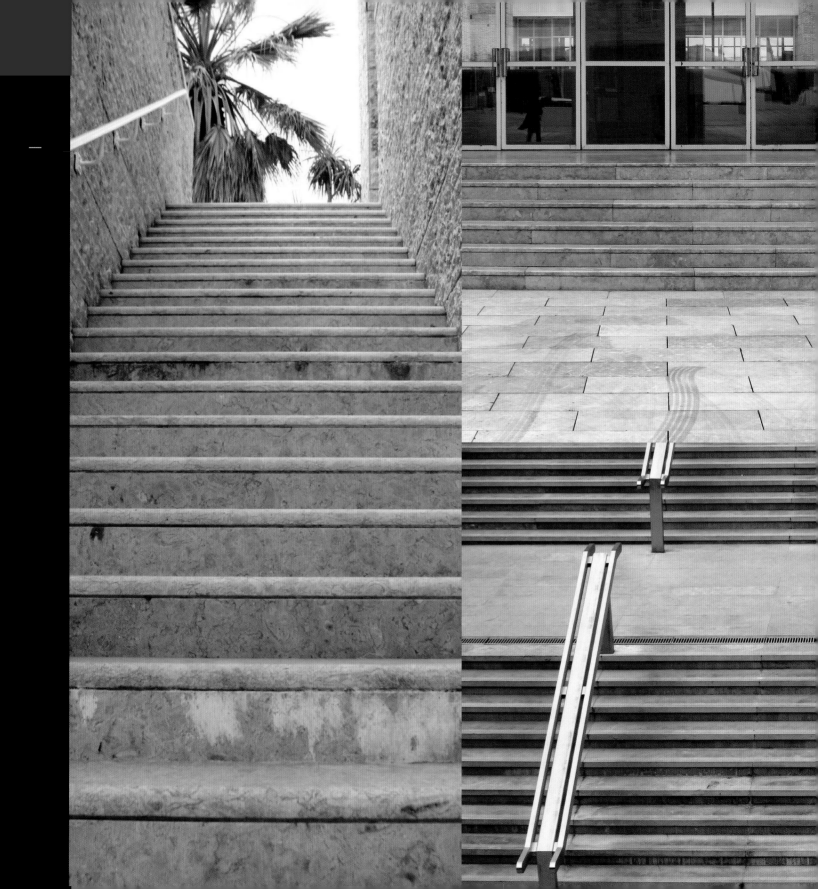

ljubljana, gosposka ulica 5

left, right: ljubljana, gosposka ulica 5 | vegova ulica 1

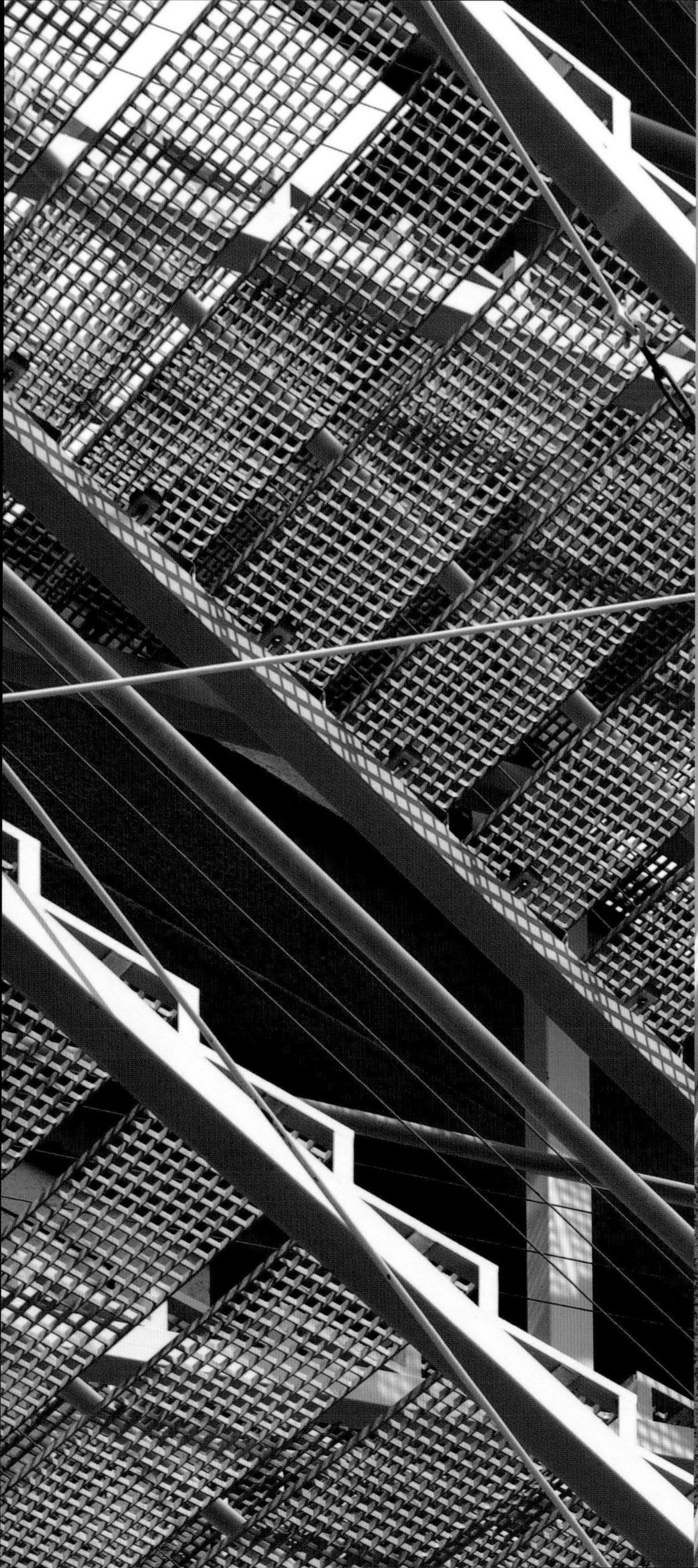

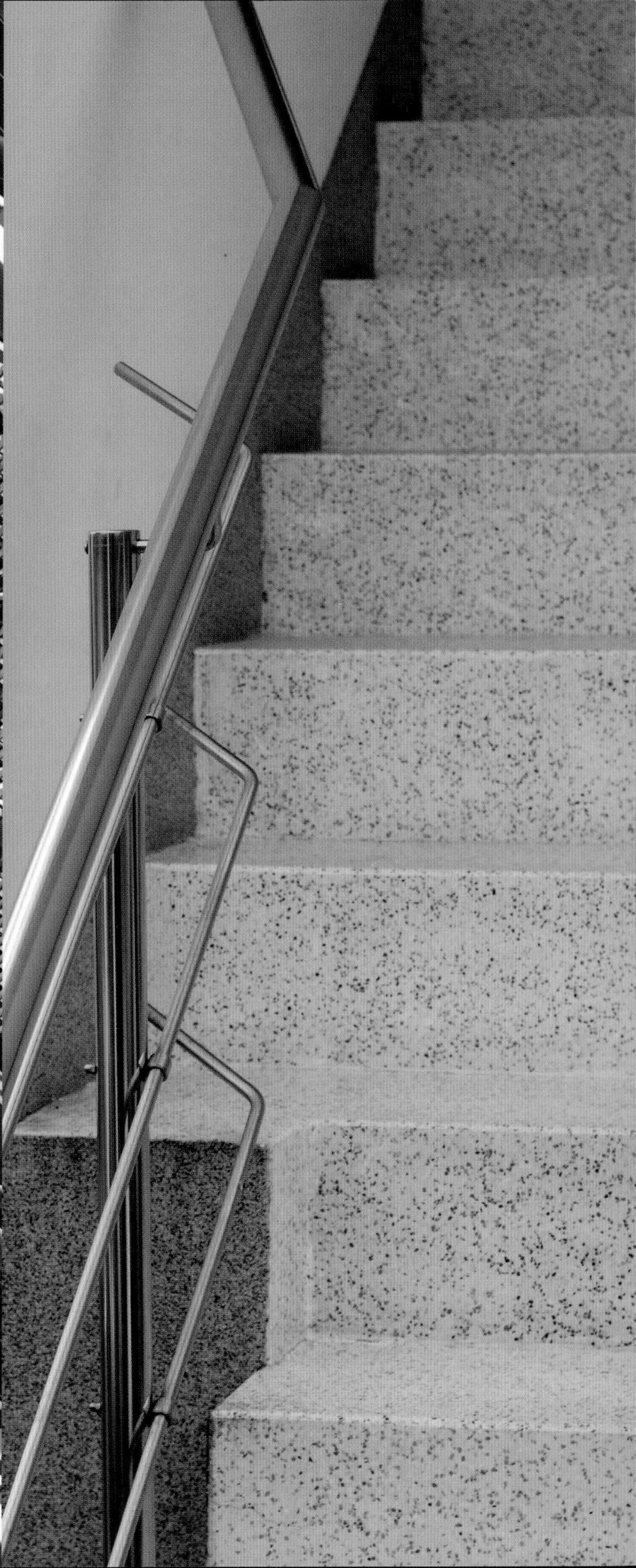

left, right: ljubljana, askerceva ulica 5 | riharjeva ulica 19

ljubljana, presernova cesta 24

ljubljana, moderna galerija

above left, above right, below left, below right: ljubljana, adamic-lundrovo nabrezje | trg republike 1 | igriska ulica 3 | gradaska ulica 20

ljubljana, gerberjevo stopnisce

london

london, city hall

left, right: london, 9-11 copper row | 1 lime street (lloyds building)

london, fulham road (brompton hospital)

london, imperial college

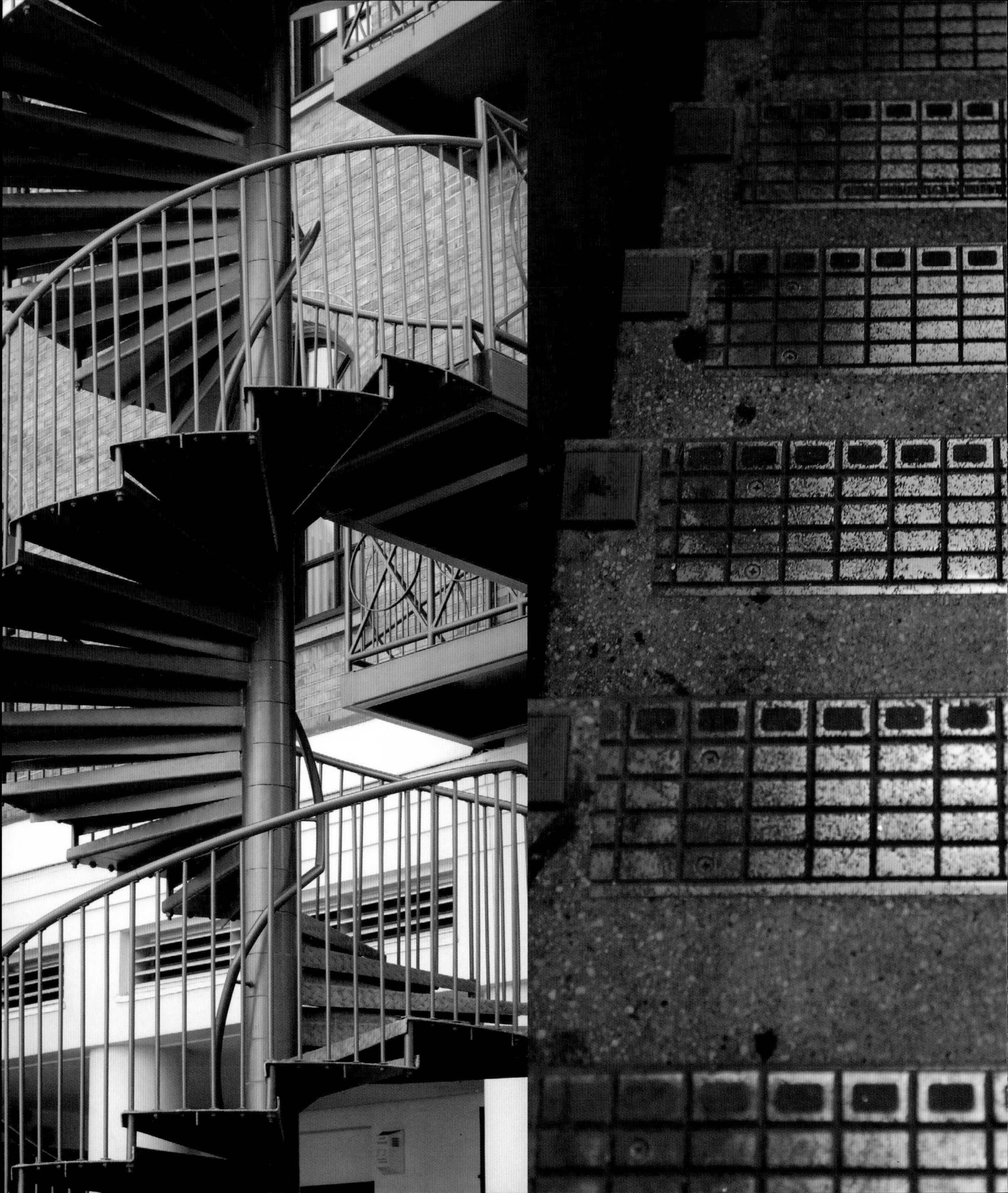

left, right: london, 5 copper row | king's cross

london, 114-130 walton street

london, thames pass

paris, parvis de la defense 1

paris, rue de mont cenis

paris, centre pompidou

above left, below left, right: paris, place jussieu 4 | louvre | esplanade de la defense

paris, place jussieu 4

prague, pražský hrad

left, above right, below right: prague, pražský hrad (matyášova brána) | pražský hrad | pražský hrad

prague, u prasneho mostu 1

prague, pražský hrad

pražský hrad

above left, above right, below left, below right: prague, u prasneho mostu 1 | radnicke schody 2 | radnicke schody 4 | u prasneho mostu 3

prague, pražský hrad

riga

riga, kronvalda bulvāris

above left, above right, below left, below right: riga, pareizticigo katedrale | jurmala | varonu ielā 3 (krematorija) | bruninieku ielā

riga, kalpaka bulvāris

rome, via labicana 144

rome, forum romanum

rome, via vittorino da feltre

stockholm

stockholm, kungliga slottet

above left, above right, below left, below right: stockholm, danderydsgatan 11 | hammargatan 4 | regeringsgatan 107 | uggleviksgatan

stockholm, malmskillnadsgatan

stockholm, kyrkogatan

st. petersburg, dumskaja ulitsa 4

ulitsa 5 | moskovski prospekt 165 (rossiiskaya natsionalnaya biblioteka) | malaja konjuschennaja ulitsa 1

st. petersburg, moskovski prospekt 161

vienna

vienna, aristide de sousa mendes promenade

above left, below left

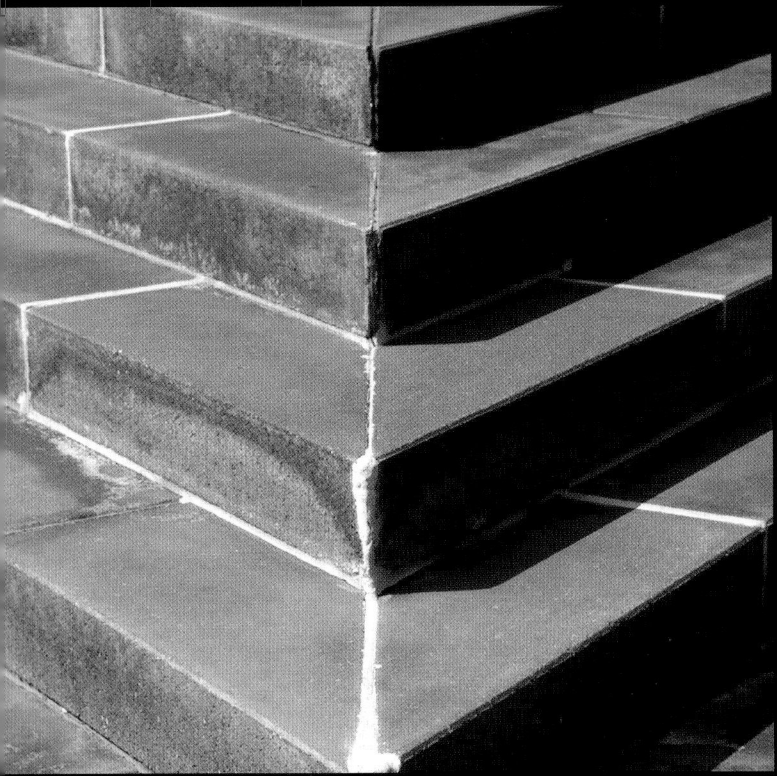

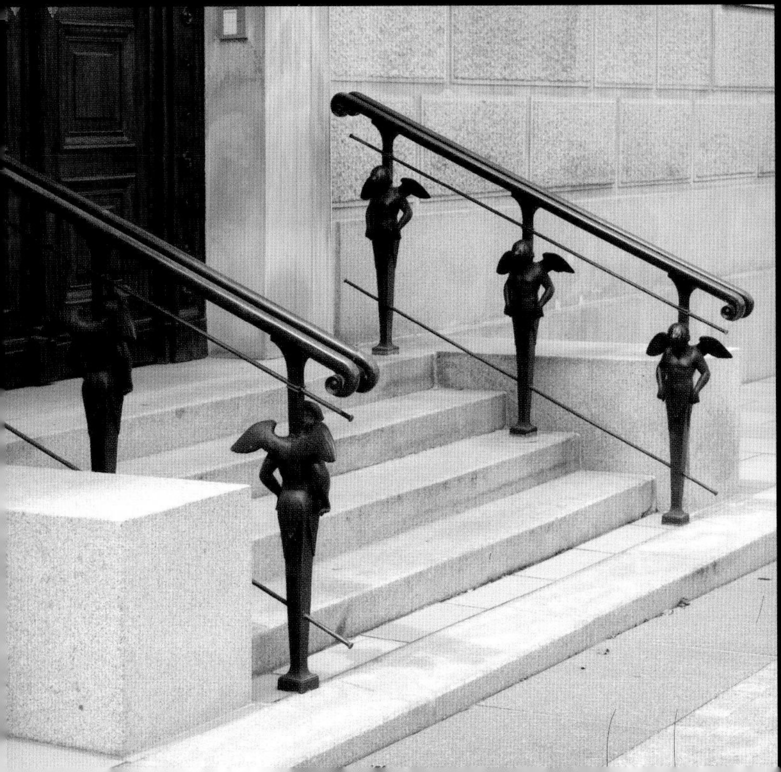

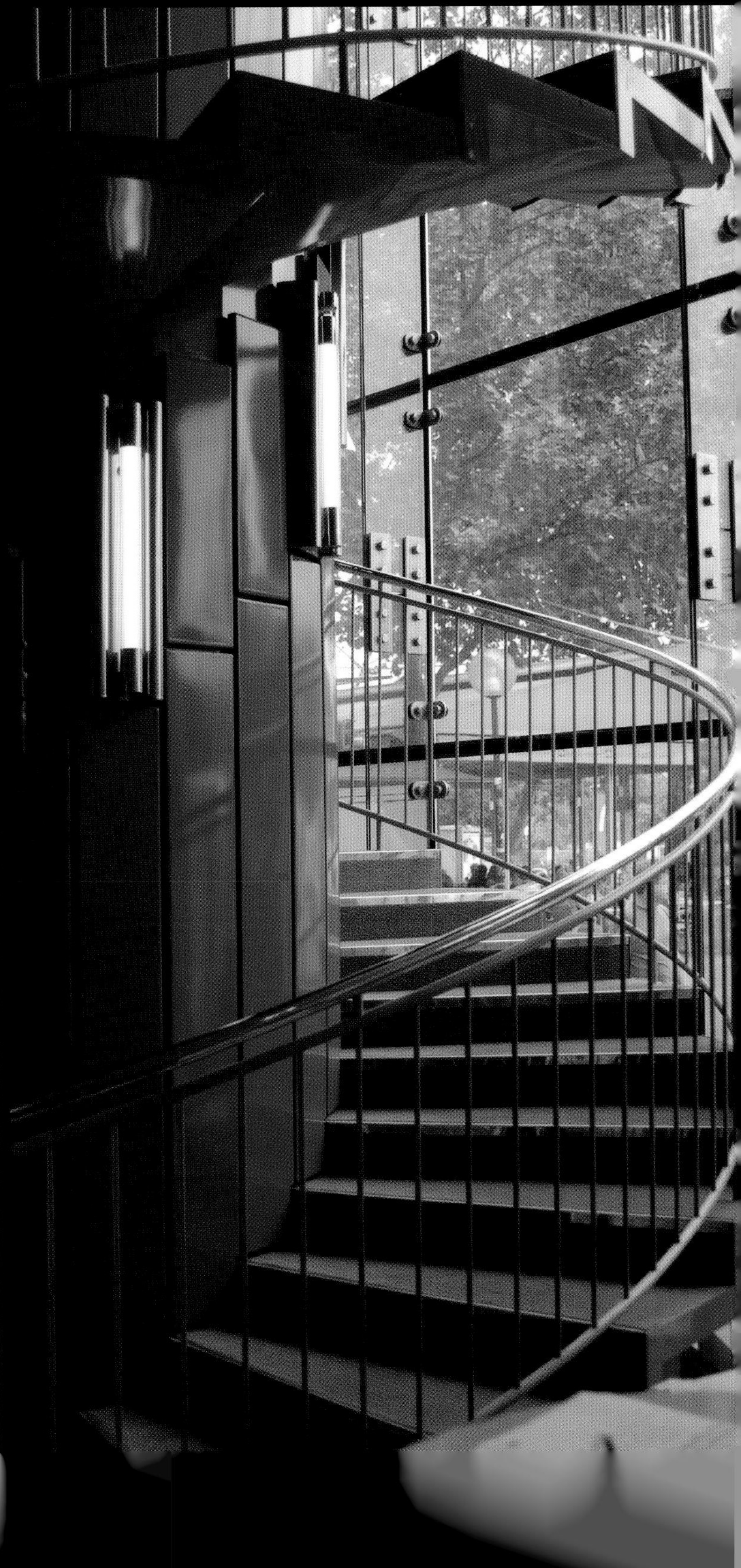

vienna, museumsplatz 1

vilnius, arkikatedra bazilika

vilnius, gedimino pospektas 51 (lietuvos nacionalinė biblioteka)

zurich, schiffbaustrasse 4

zurich, zürich-flughafen

zurich, ramistrasse 71 (universität zürich zentrum)

tannenstrasse 5

photographers index

claudia bull   st. petersburg
www.bulldesign.de

**"to photograph something you need time.
if you don't have time, you can make snapshots."**

marius flucht   amsterdam, berlin
www.herrflucht.de

"look!"

katja hoffmann   ljubljana, london, vilnius
www.katjahoffmann.de

**"without my camera I would have given up wanting to
understand the world."**

thomas kierok   barcelona, vienna, zurich
www.kierok.de

"seeing is the way to awareness."

johannes kramer   athens, budapest, prague
johannes.kramer@berlin.de

"photography for me is a confrontation with reality –
an interplay between objectivity and fantasy."

marion lammersen   paris
www.marionlammersen.com

"symbiosis of art and nature creates authentic and interesting
architecture."

bernhardt link   istanbul, rome
www.link-foto.de

"photographs reveal their own reality, or that, what the
photographer considers as such."

kai senf   berlin, brussels, copenhagen
www.kaisenf.com

"the organization and engineering of any architecture I perceive
in my viewfinder suggests a feeling of order that contrasts
the storm that is going on in my head. architecture photography
has a very meditative and calming effect on me."

claudia weidemann   lisbon, riga, stockholm
c.weidemann@berlin.de

"photography changes my perception of reality."

katja zimmermann   cracow
office@beta-75.com

**"architecture itself carries stories out of the
centuries past behind the façades – photographs of
architecture tell us completely new stories."**